TOYS

In the Past

by Joanna Brundle

©2016
Book Life
King's Lynn
Norfolk PE30 4LS

ISBN: 978-1-910512-89-0

Written by:
Joanna Brundle

Designed by:
Natalie Carr

A catalogue record for this book
is available from the British Library.

CONTENTS

You can find the red words in this book in the Glossary on page 24.

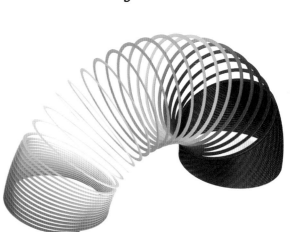

Toys from
LONG AGO

A Chinese dragon kite

Children have played with toys since time began. They play for fun, to learn, to role play and to win. People in China have enjoyed flying kites for over two thousand years.

Over five thousand years ago, the Egyptians played with stone marbles. Over two thousand years ago, the Greeks played with yo-yos and figures made of clay.

Children all over the world still enjoy playing with marbles and yo-yos.

Tudor and Victorian
TOYS

Tudor children played with skittles, a cup and ball and spinning tops. Their footballs were made from a skull or a pig's bladder.

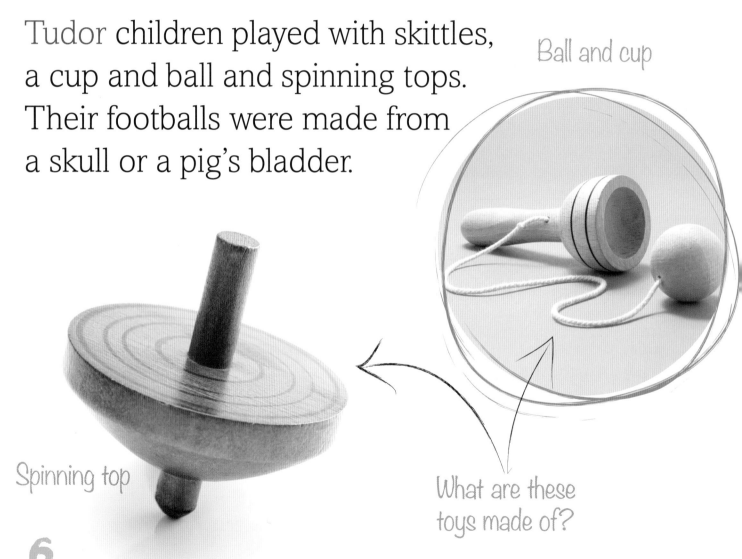

Ball and cup

Spinning top

What are these toys made of?

6

Victorian children from rich families played with rocking horses, dolls, toy soldiers and model trains. Only toys based on Bible stories, like Noah's Ark, were allowed on Sundays.

A doll

A rocking horse

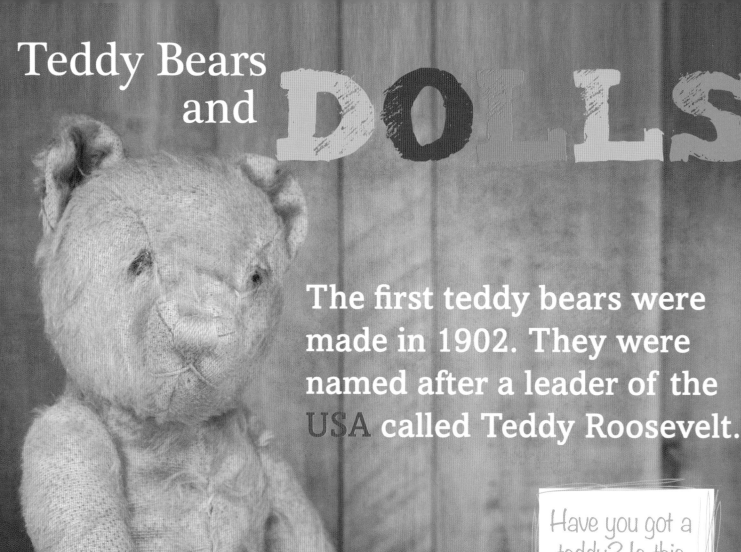

Teddy Bears and DOLLS

The first teddy bears were made in 1902. They were named after a leader of the USA called Teddy Roosevelt.

Have you got a teddy? Is this old bear different from yours?

Long ago, dolls were made of clay or wood.
Victorian dolls were made of china.
The first talking doll was made in 1823.

Wooden Russian dolls were
first made in 1890.

Playing OUTSIDE

Children have played with toy scooters and pedal cars for over one hundred years. The bicycle became popular in Victorian times.

An old toy scooter

Children used to play in the streets. There were few vehicles so it was safer to play. They played with skipping ropes, a whip and top and conkers.

Conkers

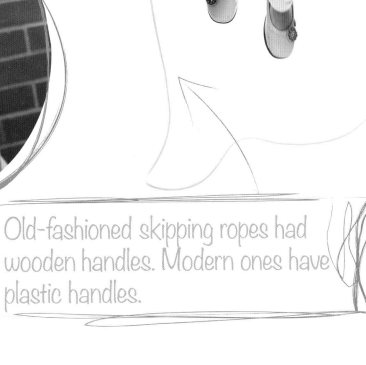

Old-fashioned skipping ropes had wooden handles. Modern ones have plastic handles.

Toys for BOYS

People used to think some toys were only for boys and some were only for girls. Boys played with trains and toy soldiers and games like football and rugby.

Toy soldiers

Toys for GIRLS

Dolls pram

Girls were expected to play quietly with dolls prams, toy tea sets or games like Ludo. Now, boys and girls play with all sorts of toys.

Parents' and Grandparents' TOYS

Your parents played with roller skates, action figures like Barbie or Action Man or toys based on television programmes like Dr Who. Your grandparents liked Meccano, Snakes and Ladders and jigsaws.

Barbies

Ask whoever looks after you what their favourite toys were.

Clockwork car

Your grandparents may have played with clockwork cars or trains. Mummy or Daddy probably had an electric train set or racing car.

CRAZES

A craze happens when a toy becomes so popular that everyone wants one. Television programmes and films, like Toy Story, have sometimes started crazes.

Yo-Yo

Trading cards

Do you play with any toys that belonged to whoever looks after you?

Most crazes disappear but some, like skateboards, are still played with today. Why do you think some crazes last?

How can We Tell how
OLD TOYS ARE?

Looking at what a toy is made from can help us to tell how old it is. A rusty metal car is probably older than a plastic one.

Plastic truck

Metal car

Some old toys may look new because they belong
to collectors who take care of them.

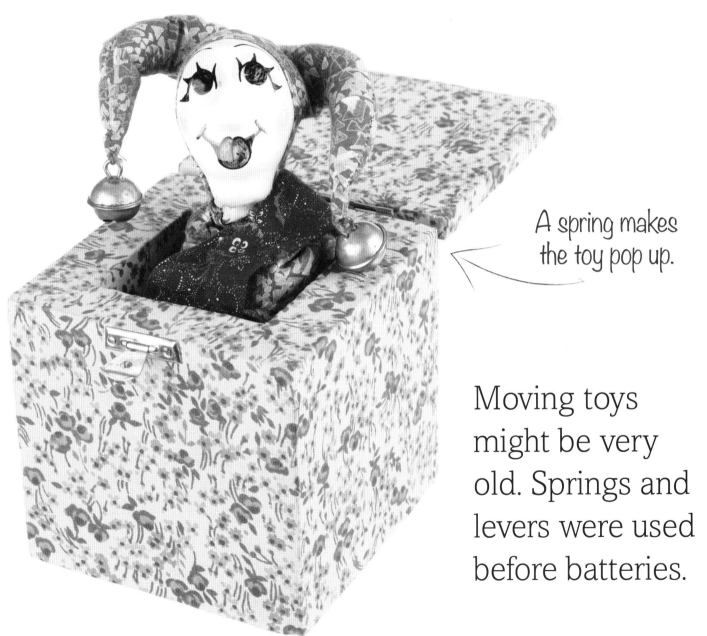

A spring makes
the toy pop up.

Moving toys
might be very
old. Springs and
levers were used
before batteries.

19

TIMELINE

1767
The first jigsaw was made.

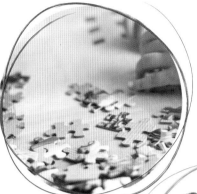

1919
The pogo stick was invented.

1949
Lego went on sale.

1957
The frisbee was invented.

1959
Barbie appeared.

1990'S

Rollerblades and Beanie Babies were crazes.

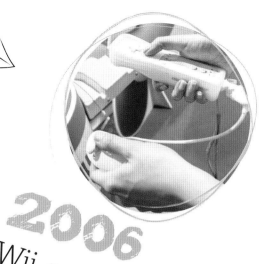

2006

Wii computer games were invented.

1980'S

Nintendo appeared.

1970'S

The first computer games were made.

1960'S

Twister and Operation went on sale.

FUN FACTS

1 Barbie's real name is Barbara Millicent Roberts.

Children playing with Barbies

Slinky

2 It takes over 19 metres of wire to make a Slinky.

3 The first video game was called Pong. It was based on ping pong.

Hula Hoops

4 Monopoly is the most played board game in the world.

5 More than 20 million hula hoops were sold in the first 6 months.

GLOSSARY

CLAY
A sticky, natural material that dries hard

COLLECTORS
People who enjoy collecting groups of things, like toys

EGYPTIANS
People who lived in Egypt thousands of years ago

GREEKS
People who lived in Greece thousands of years ago

MONOPOLY
A game in which you try to get other players' money

ROLE-PLAY
Pretending to be someone else

TUDOR
A person who lived when the Tudors were the ruling family of England from 1485-1603

USA
The United States of America, one of the largest countries in the world

VICTORIAN
A person who lived when Victoria was Queen from 1837-1901

Photocredits: Abbreviations: l-left, r-right, b-bottom, t-top, c-centre, m-middle. All images are courtesy of Shutterstock.com.
Front Cover, 1 – Elena Schweitzer. 2 – Ivonne Wierink. 3b – Kellis. 3rt – kai keisuke. 3rb – AlexLMX. 4 – Tom Wang. 45- auremar. 6 l – kai keisuke. 6r – HomeStudio. 7l – Dario Lo Presti. 7r – Elzbieta Sekowska. 8 – Robyn Mackenzie. 9 -Tatiana Popova. 10 – Elzbieta Sekowska. 11l – Peter Elvidge. 11r – Olga Sapegina. 12 – Vtldtlm. 13 – Anneka. 14l – photosync. 14r – Stefano Tinti. 15tr – Benjamin Mercer. 15 – Claudia Otte. 16l – Sergei Bachlakov. 16r – joppo. 17 – lzf. 18l – maxstockphoto. 18r – Viktor1. 19 – mutation. 20mt – berna namoglu. 20ml – KPG Ivary. 20mr – Hurst Photo. 20bl – pirita. 20br – netsuthep. 21tl – Kamila Starzycka. 21tr – Stefano Tinti. 21m – CTR Photos. 21bl – digitalreflections. 21br – millatiger. 22t – Stefano Tinti. 22b – AlexLMX. 23tl – Darren Pullman. 23lm – 2xSamara.com. 23br – CaseyMartin.